J R558797
599.5 17.27
Wol
Wolpert
Whale magic for kids

DATE DUE			
JE 17 '9		SE 08 '93	SE 20 '95
FE 12 '93		JY 18 '94	SE 30 '95
JY 2 '93		SE 16 '94	
JY 24 '93		NO 16 '94	
	NO 26 '93	JA 07 '95	
JA 7 '94			
MY 28 '94		MR 18 '95	
		JY 10 '95	
JE 25 '94		AG 14 '95	

RF

GREAT RIVER REGIONAL LIBRARY
St. Cloud, Minnesota 56301

T5-ADA-643

by Tom Wolpert

WHALES
Whale Magic for Kids

Gareth Stevens Children's Books
MILWAUKEE

For a free color catalog describing Gareth Stevens' list of high-quality children's books, call 1-800-341-3569 (USA) or 1-800-461-9120 (Canada).

Library of Congress Cataloging-in-Publication Data

Wolpert, Tom.
    Whale magic for kids / by Tom Wolpert.
        p. cm. — (Animal magic for kids)
    Includes index.
    Summary: Discusses the different kinds of whales, their behavior and habitat.
    ISBN 0-8368-0660-3
    1. Whales—Juvenile literature. [1. Whales.] I. Title. II. Series.
QL737.C4W65   1991
599.5—dc20   90-50718

This North American edition published by
Gareth Stevens Children's Books
1555 North RiverCenter Drive, Suite 201
Milwaukee, Wisconsin 53212, USA

First published in 1990 by NorthWord Press, Inc., with a text by Tom Wolpert.
Copyright © 1990 by NorthWord Press, Inc.

All rights reserved. No part of this book may be reproduced or used in any form or by any means without permission in writing from Gareth Stevens, Inc.

Printed in the United States of America

1 2 3 4 5 6 7 8 9 9 97 96 95 94 93 92 91

Whales swim the oceans of the world. They dive to great depths and cruise the sunny waves as they please. That's because they are the largest animals that ever lived.

The blue whale, for instance, may grow 90 feet long and weigh 300,000 pounds. In fact, a dinosaur, an elephant and a man could fit on a blue whale's back with room to spare.

Whales may look like fish, but they are not fish at all. Whales are *mammals* — just like dogs, cats, cows and human beings.

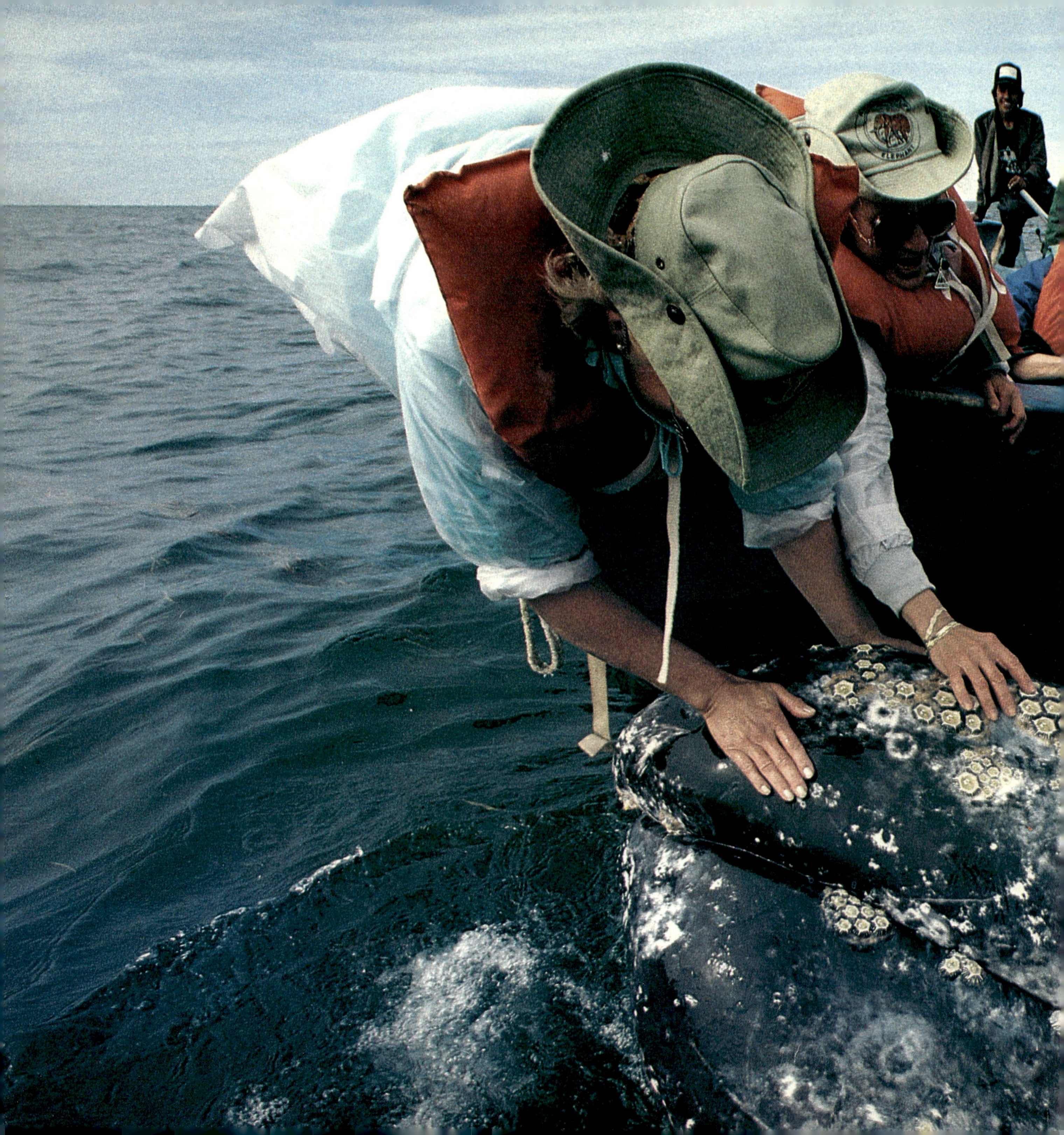

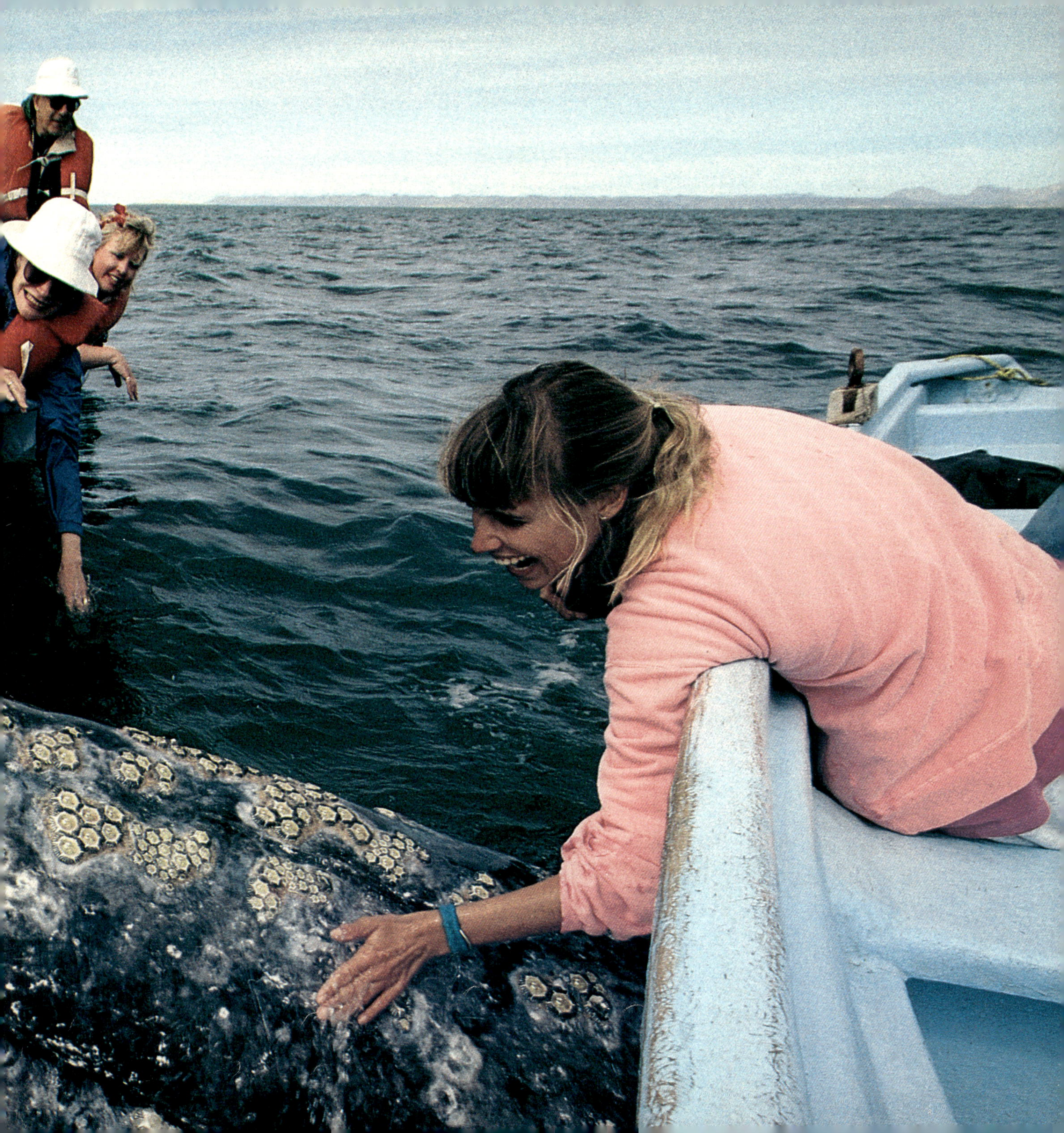

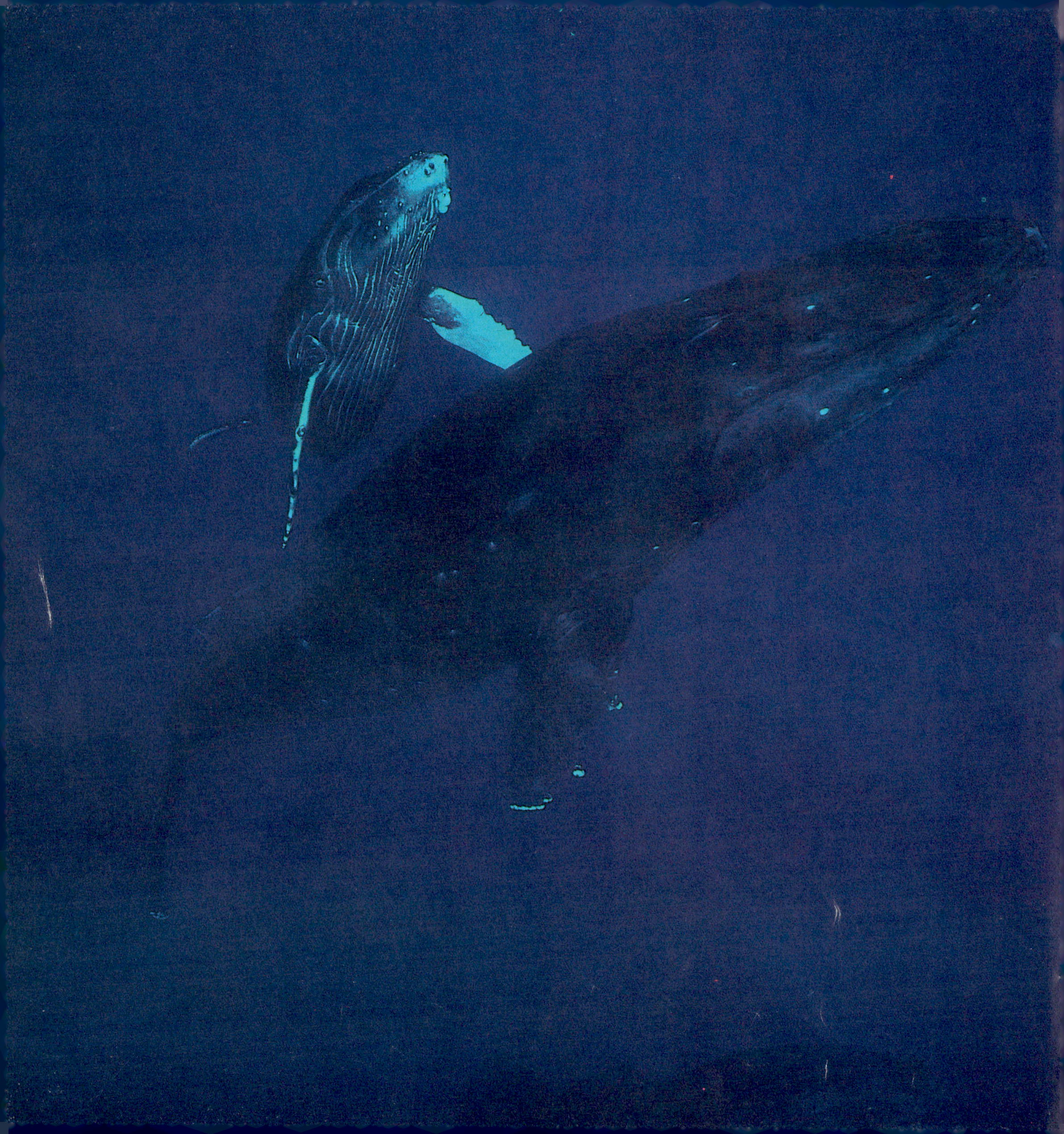

Because they are mammals, whales give birth to their young alive (fish lay eggs). Baby whales nurse on their mother's milk (young fish do not nurse at all). Whales breathe through lungs and must hold their breath (fish breathe through gills).

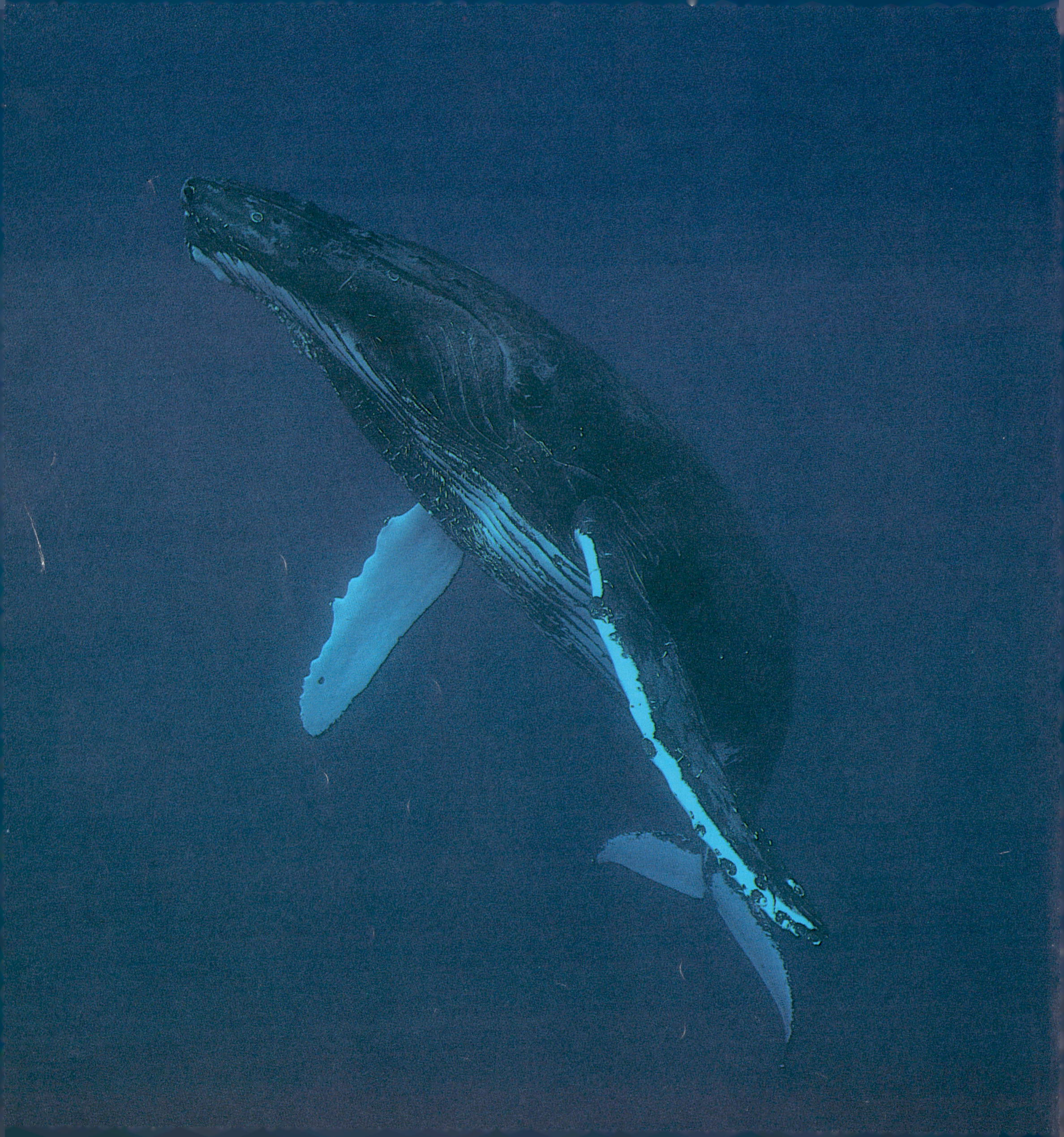

But whales are also very different from most mammals. For example, compare yourself to a whale. You can smell with your nose (a whale has no sense of smell). You hear with ears (a whale can hear but has no real ears – only tiny ear openings). You have four limbs – two legs and two arms (a whale has only two front limbs called *flippers*). So, even though humans and whales are both mammals, they are very different from one another.

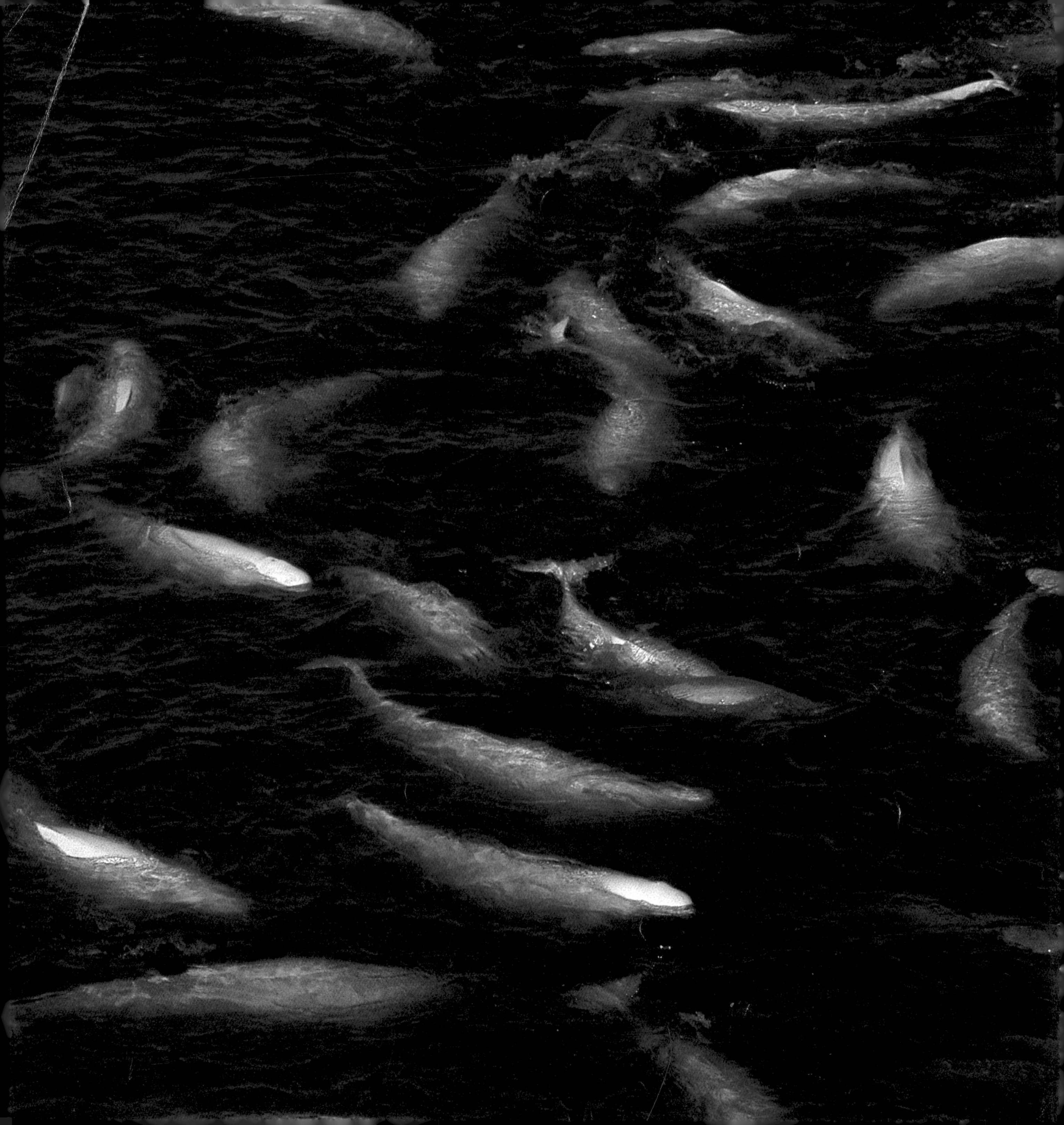

Some types of whales feed and travel in groups which sometimes number hundreds of whales. These large groups are called herds or pods. Other whales travel in small family groups of two or three animals. A family group may include a bull (adult male); a cow (adult female); and a calf (a baby or immature whale).

Female whales carry their young inside their bodies for up to eighteen months before giving birth. When born, calves do not have enough *blubber* to float. Mother whales keep their calves in constant motion to help them breathe.

After one month, the calves have developed enough blubber to float and swim without help. They now spend most of their time playing and learning to turn, roll, dive and touch. Sometimes when a calf becomes too playful the mother hugs it against her stomach with her flippers until the calf calms down.

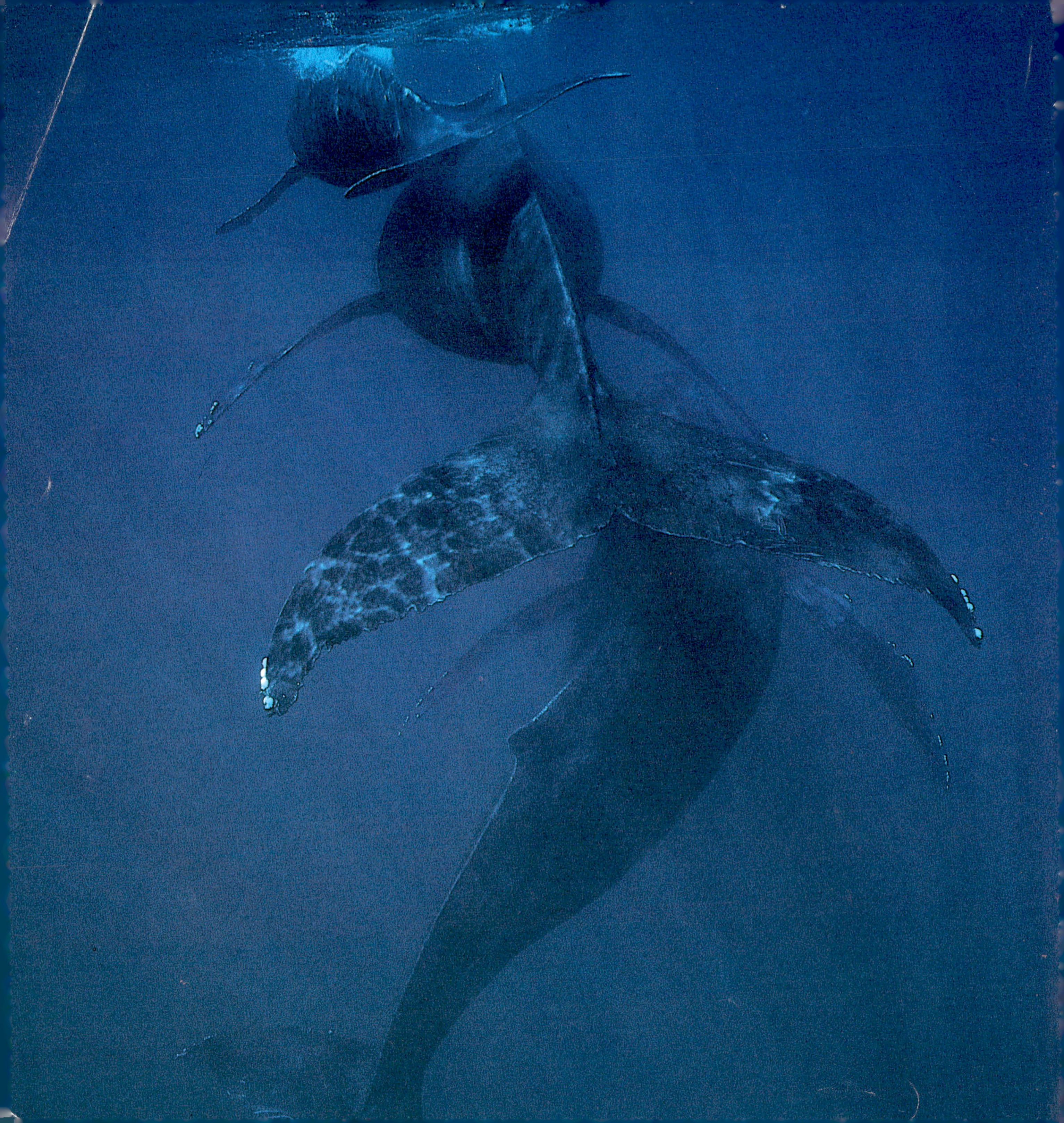

Whales swim by thrusting their powerful tail fins up and down. These fins are called *flukes*. Their flippers are used only for balance and turning. Most whales swim at a speed of three to five miles per hour. However, blue and killer whales can go as fast as 25 miles per hour!

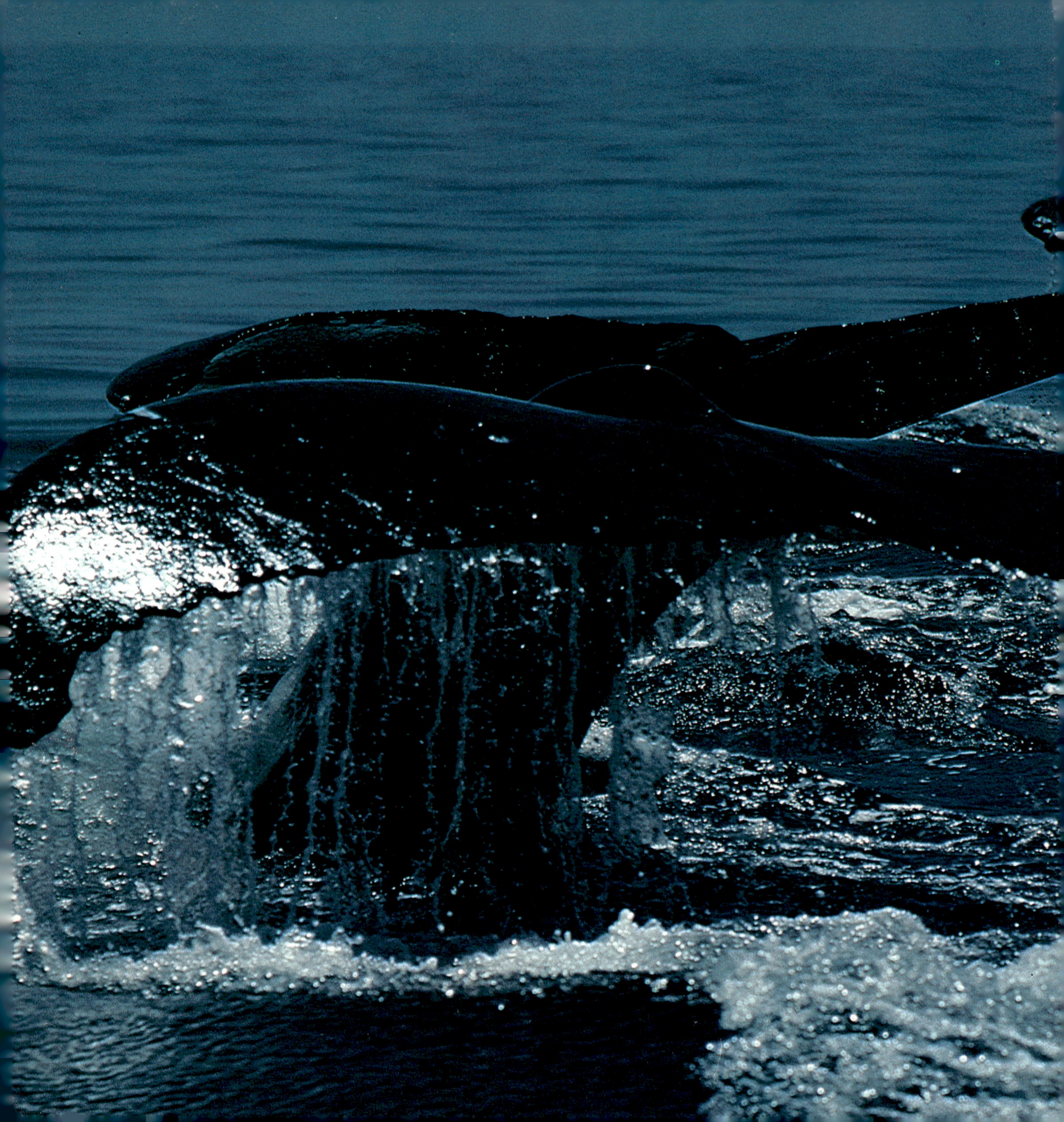

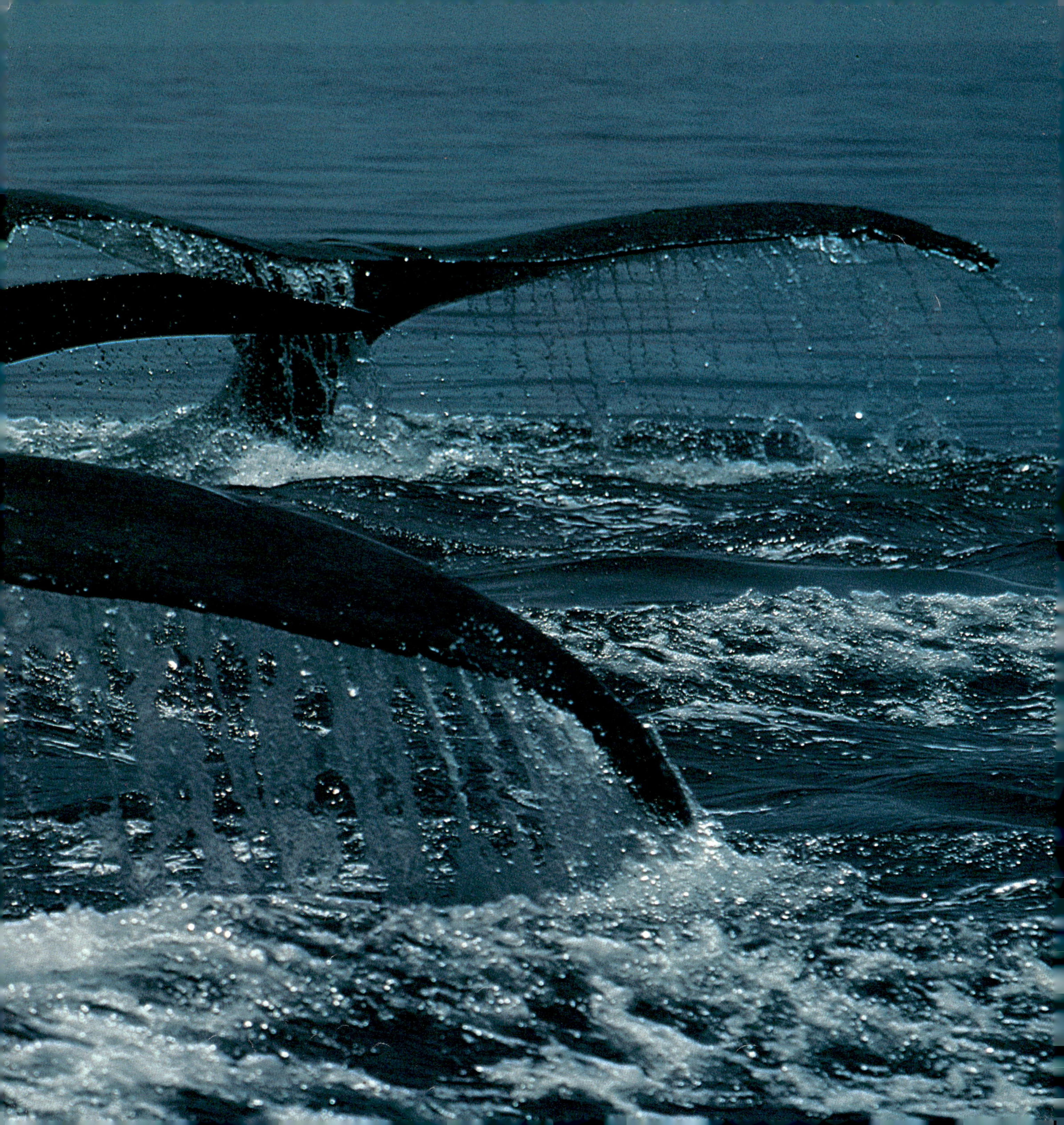

Adult whales will use their size and power to protect their young. Whales have only one enemy other than man. That enemy is the killer whale. Whales do not, as far as we know, fight among themselves, and whales seldom attack boats unless they have been wounded.

Whales swim or dive most of the time. They produce an oily substance to protect their eyes from the salty ocean water. Whales depend on their sense of hearing more than their sense of sight. Sound travels faster through the water than through air, and this is important to whales since they have excellent hearing. Whales do not sleep for long periods of time, but take naps for a few minutes at a time at the surface of the water.

Even though whales breathe air, they would die on land. If a whale is stranded on land, the great weight of its body presses down on its lungs and the whale eventually *suffocates*. It needs the water to support its huge body.

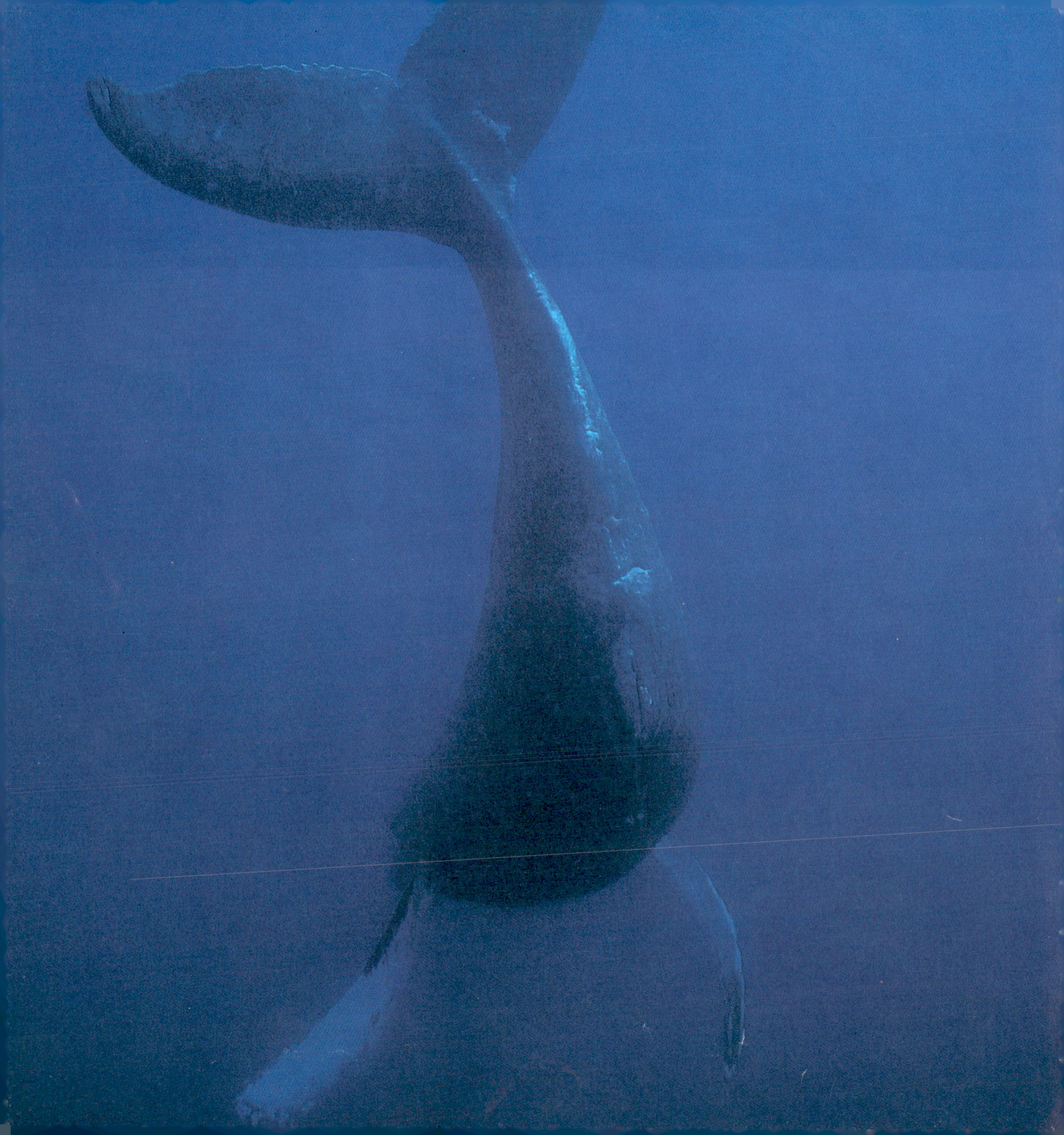

As you can guess, whales have pretty big appetites. Larger whales eat nearly a ton of food daily. When whales dive for food, the air in their lungs becomes hot and moist from body heat. Upon reaching the surface, they blow the air out through a hole in the top of their head. The hot breath strikes the cold air outside and *condenses* to form a spout of fog.

These fog spouts, or "blows", alert people to the presence of whales from great distances. Most people wish only to observe the gentle, even friendly, whales. Others, however, are commercial hunters who kill whales for their meat, hide and body oil.

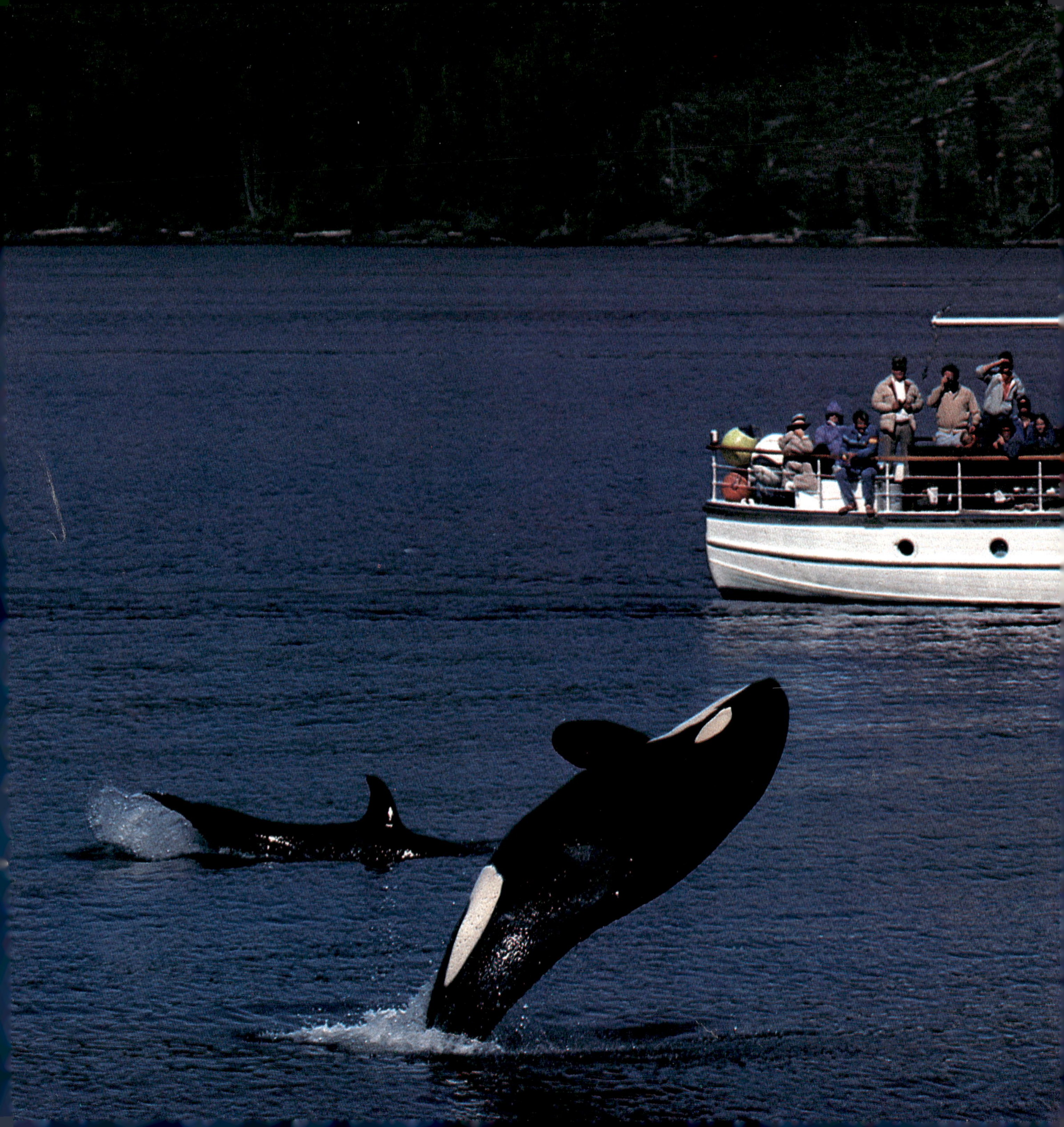

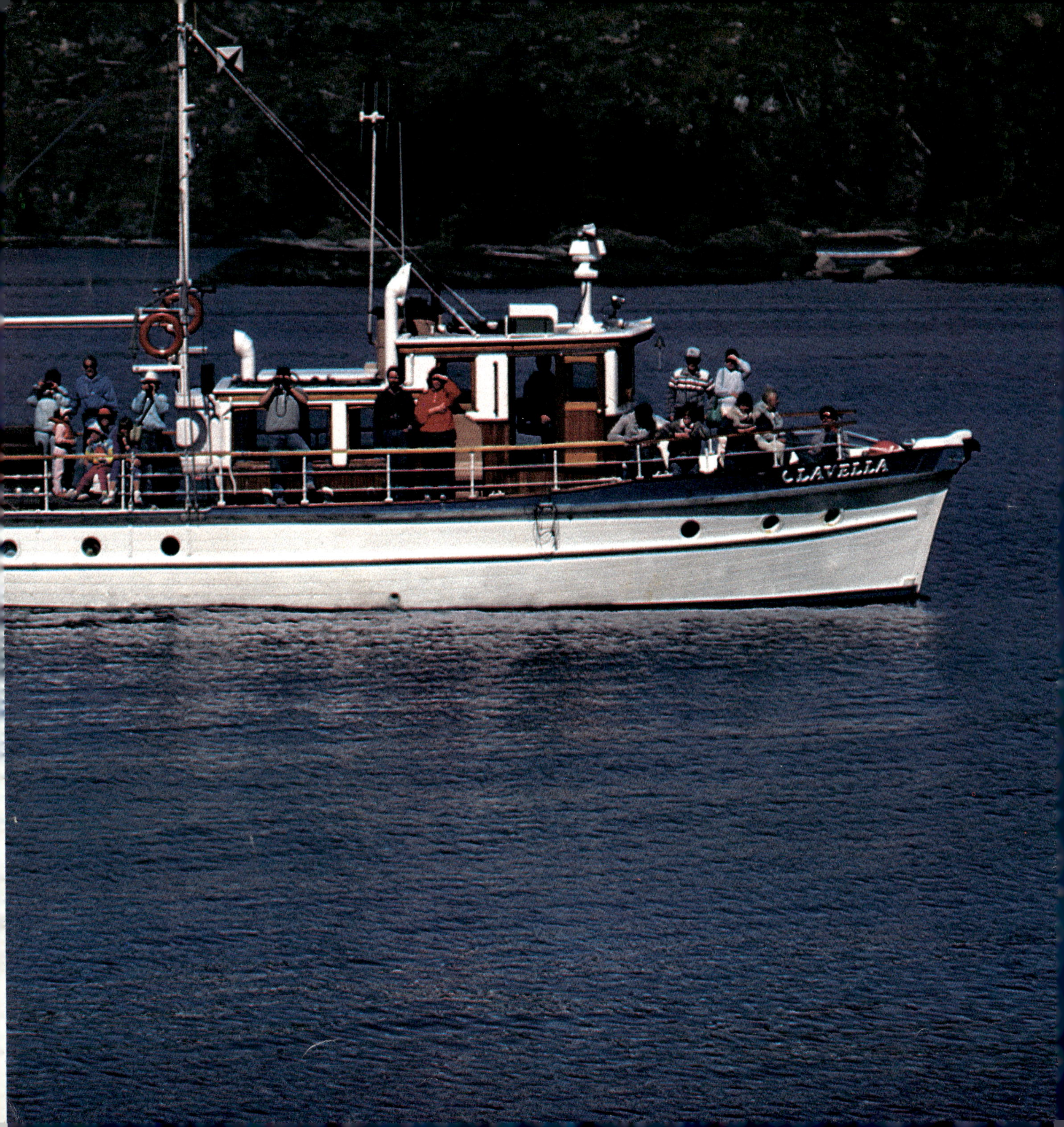
CLAVELLA

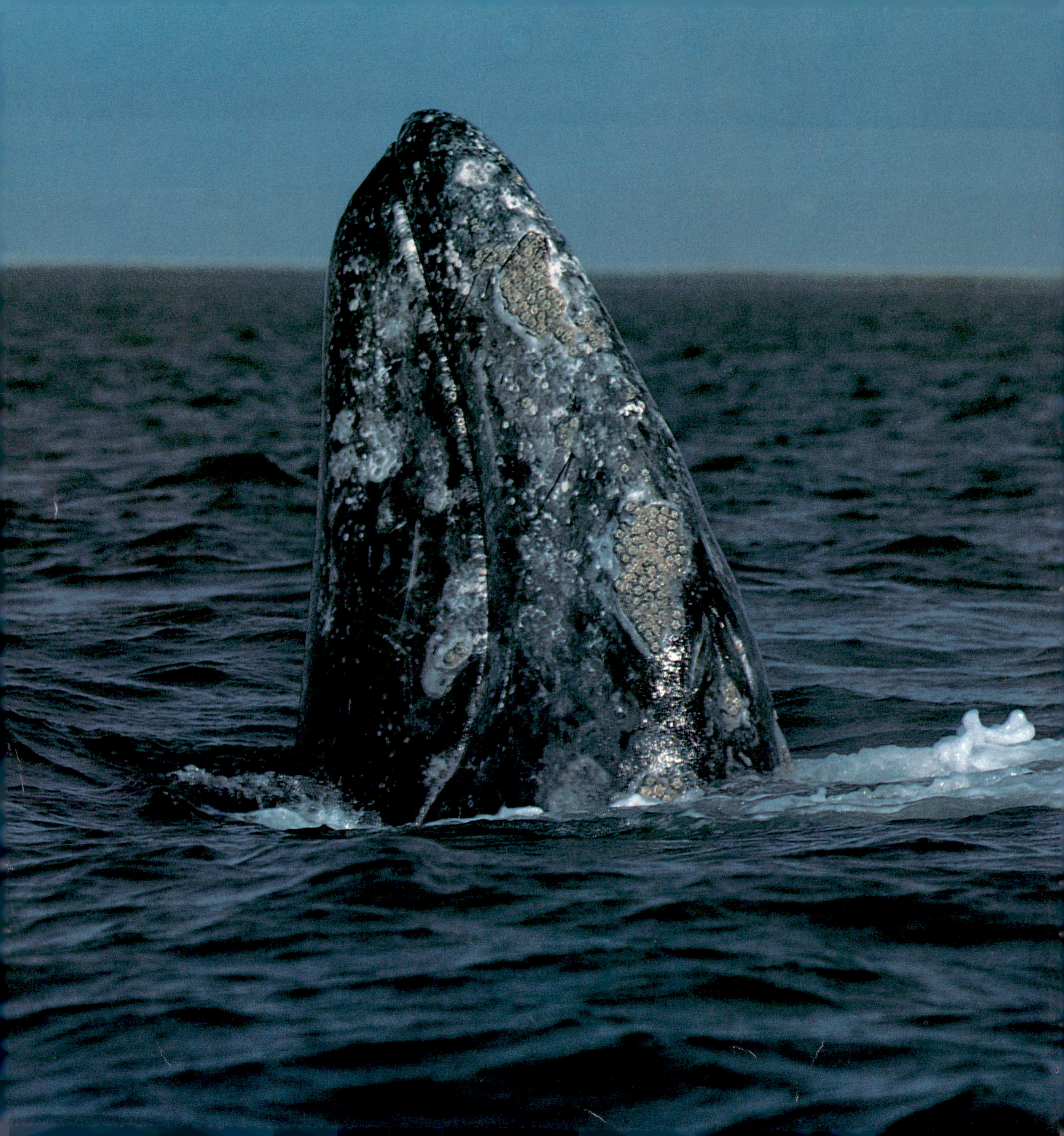

Some whales were once hunted nearly to *extinction*. Fortunately, the majority of people and their governments today wish to save and protect whales throughout the world. Someday the whales may cruise the sunny waves without harm from humans at all. That will be good news for whales and whale-lovers like you and me.

The *origins* of the whale date back about sixty million years (60,000,000) to members of a family of early mammals known as *mesonychids*. Mesonychids were some of nature's earliest designs for life on earth. They had four legs and a tail. They were furry, carried their babies inside their bodies until birth and nursed their young.

Some of these early mammals lived along the shores of swamps and *estuaries*. They probably walked along the beaches searching for food.

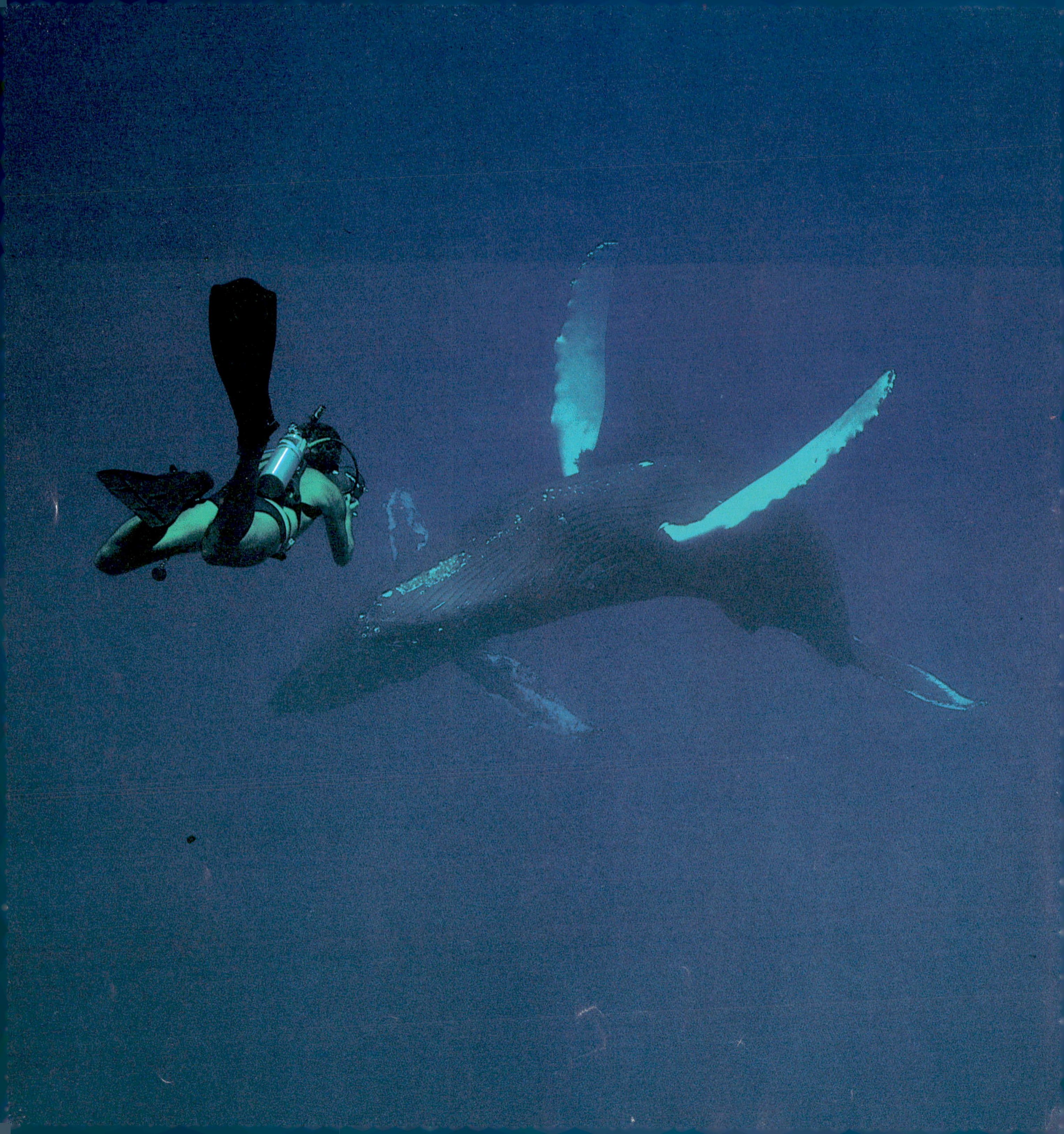

Eventually, some began wading in the water in search of food. They would hold their breath to duck their heads under the water to gather food. As they waded deeper, they found more food. Soon some began to dive and swim in the shallows.

The longer they stayed at sea the better they fared. The sea provided a plentiful supply of food. Over a long period of time they found that all their needs could be met in the sea. They had no reason to return to land. These land mammals evolved, over thousands of years, into sea animals. They *adapted* to a new environment.

Once at sea they gradually took the shape of fish. Today, whales are so well adapted to life underwater that it is easy to forget they were once mammals of the land. Remember, this change from land life to sea life took place thousands of years ago.

Not all mesonychids became sea mammals. Many survived well with the food available on land. In time these mammals evolved into modern *artiodactyls*. We know this kind of animal as the antelope, buffalo, caribou, cow, pig, moose, and musk-ox.

Probably the land mammal that is most closely related to the whale is the hippopotamus. It is surprising to think of the whale and hippopotamus as being related, but they are.

The Toothed Whales
Toothed whales eat fish and squids. Although they can hold their prey in their peg-like teeth, they swallow their food whole without chewing it. A sperm whale could easily swallow a man.

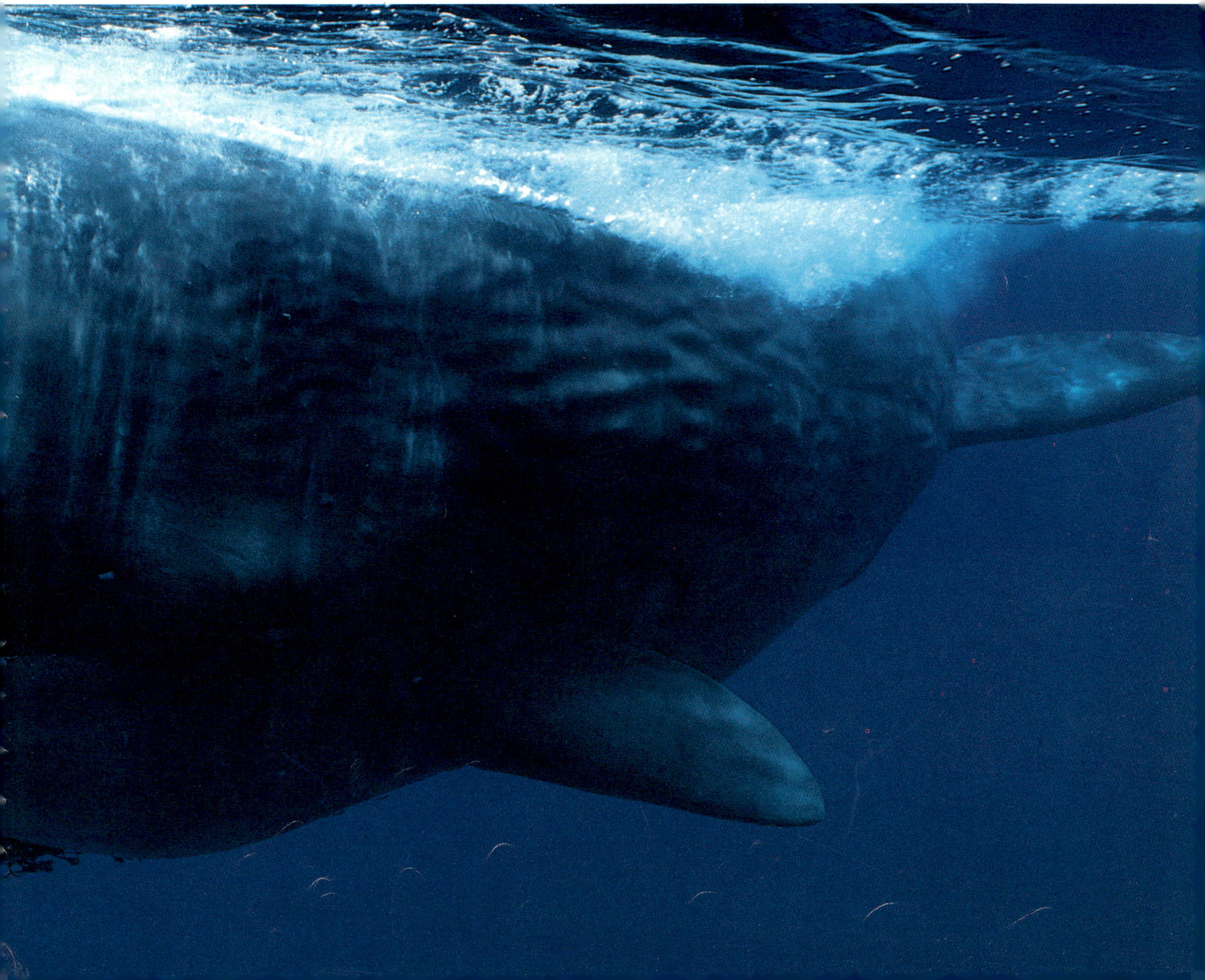

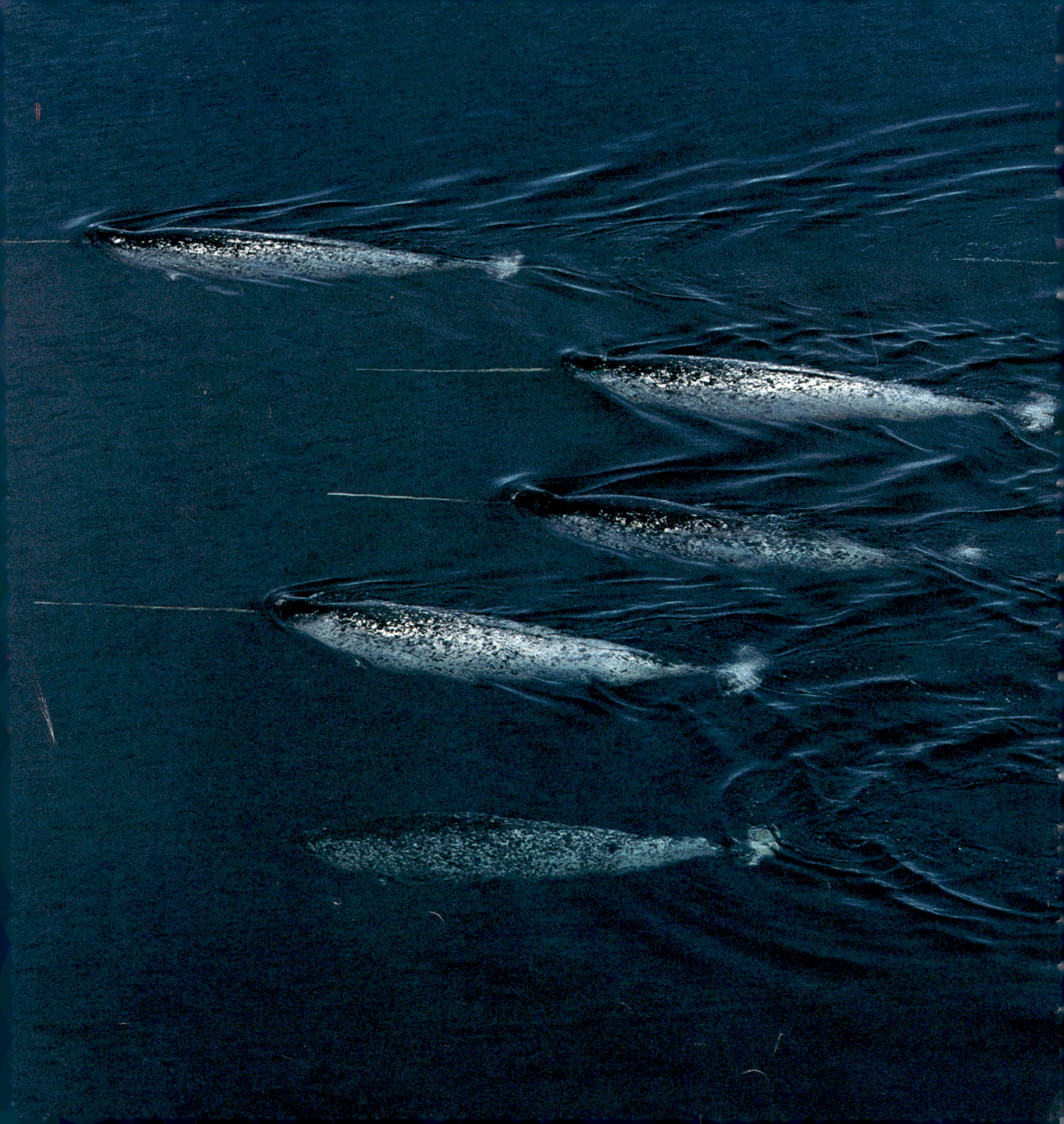

Sperm Whale:
Maximum length - 65 feet
Weight - 60 tons (120,000 lbs.)

Characteristics: The sperm whale is the largest toothed whale. It has 35 to 65 teeth. Its enormous head makes up one-third of the body length. The head contains an enormous amount of "spermaceti," a waxy material used in cosmetics. This is one reason it is still hunted and killed. A sperm whale is dark gray and may be found in all oceans.

Narwhal Whale:
Maximum length - 18 feet
Weight - 2 tons (4,000 lbs.)

Characteristics: The male narwhal whale has a spiral ivory tusk about eight feet long jutting from the left side of its head. The female narwhal has no tusk. The narwhal is gray-white with dark gray or black spots on its skin and is found in arctic regions.

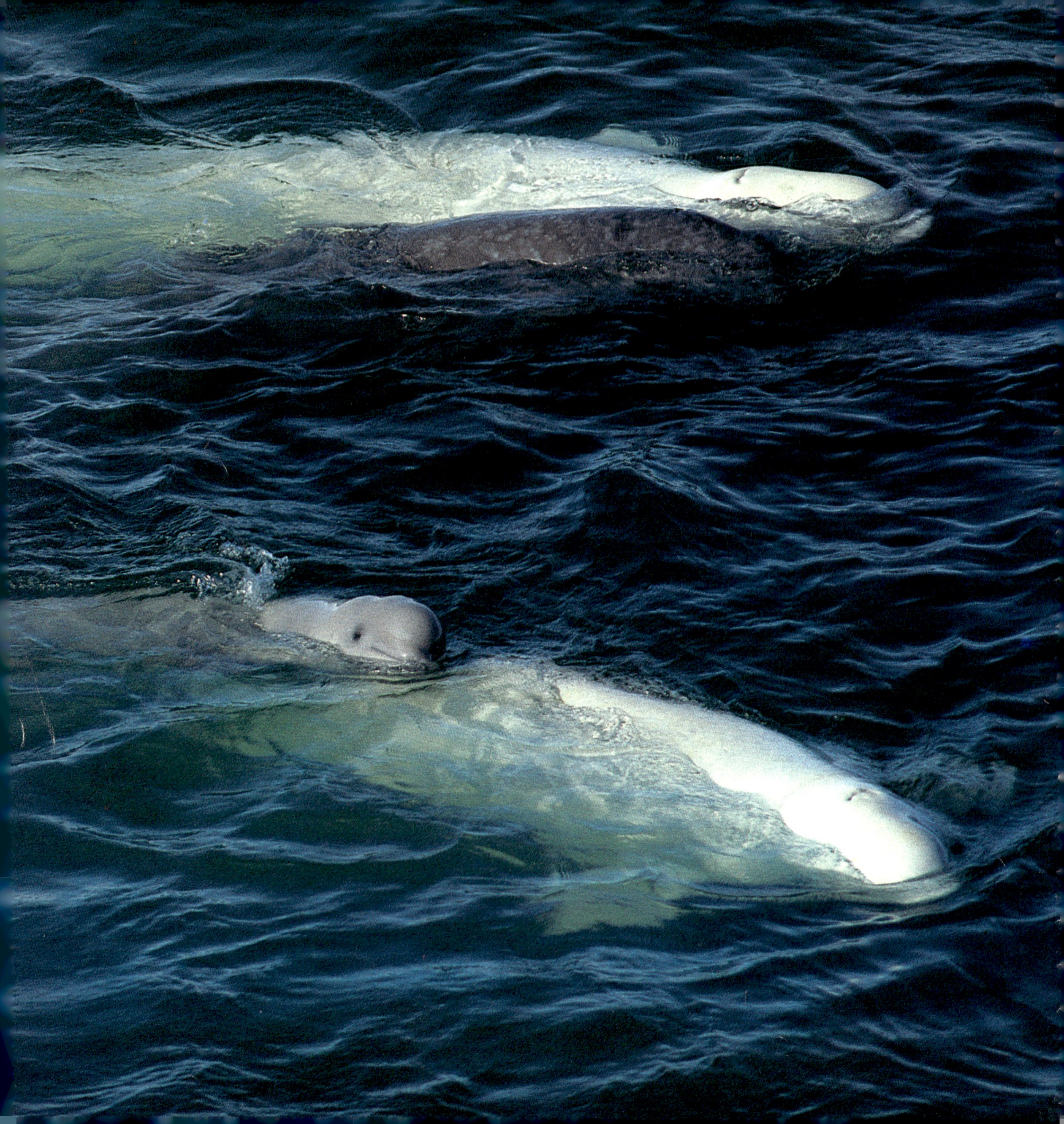

Bottle Nose Whale:
Maximum length - 30 feet
Weight - 30 tons (60,000 lbs.)

Characteristics: The bottle nose whale has four teeth. Its forehead has a distinctive swelling. The bottle nose whale is dark in color and lives in the North Atlantic and Antarctic regions.

Giant Bottle Nose Whale:
Maximum length – 42 feet
Weight – 30 tons (60,000 lbs.)

Characteristics: The giant bottle nose whale has four teeth. Its snout narrows into a round "beak" – like the neck of a bottle. The giant bottle nose whale is black or dark gray in color and lives in the north Pacific and Antarctic regions.

Killer Whale:

Maximum length - 30 feet
Weight - 10 tons (20,000 lbs.)

Characteristics: The killer whale has a glossy black back and a white underside. It has 40-48 teeth — ten to twelve teeth on each side, upper and lower, on each jaw. Killer whales travel in groups of two to dozens and can travel up to 25 miles per hour. They primarily eat salmon and other large fish. However, they sometimes attack porpoises, seals, walruses and newborn whales. Killer whales are found in all oceans but especially in cold regions.

The Baleen Whales

Baleen whales eat *plankton*, which are small sea animals and plants. When a baleen whale approaches, a mass of plankton flow in. Then closing its mouth, the whale's tongue squeezes out the water leaving only the nutritious plankton.

Some Baleen Whales:

Blue Whale:
Maximum length - 95 feet
Weight - 150 tons (300,000 lbs.)

Characteristics: The blue whale is the largest and fastest-swimming whale. It is bluish in color except for yellow on its underside caused by a coating of tiny water plants. It is found in all oceans.

Finback Whale:
Maximum length - 82 feet
Weight - 100 tons (200,000 lbs.)

Characteristics: The finback whale has a prominent fin on its back and a slender body. It has a gray-black back, a white underside, and a white patch on front of the right upper jaw. It is found in all oceans.

Sei Whale:
Maximum length - 55 feet
Weight - 40 tons (80,000 lbs.)

Characteristics: The sei whale looks very similar to a finback whale, but is has no white patch on its jaw. Like the finback whale, it also has a prominent fin on its back. The sei whale has a dark back and a light underside. The sei whale is found in all oceans.

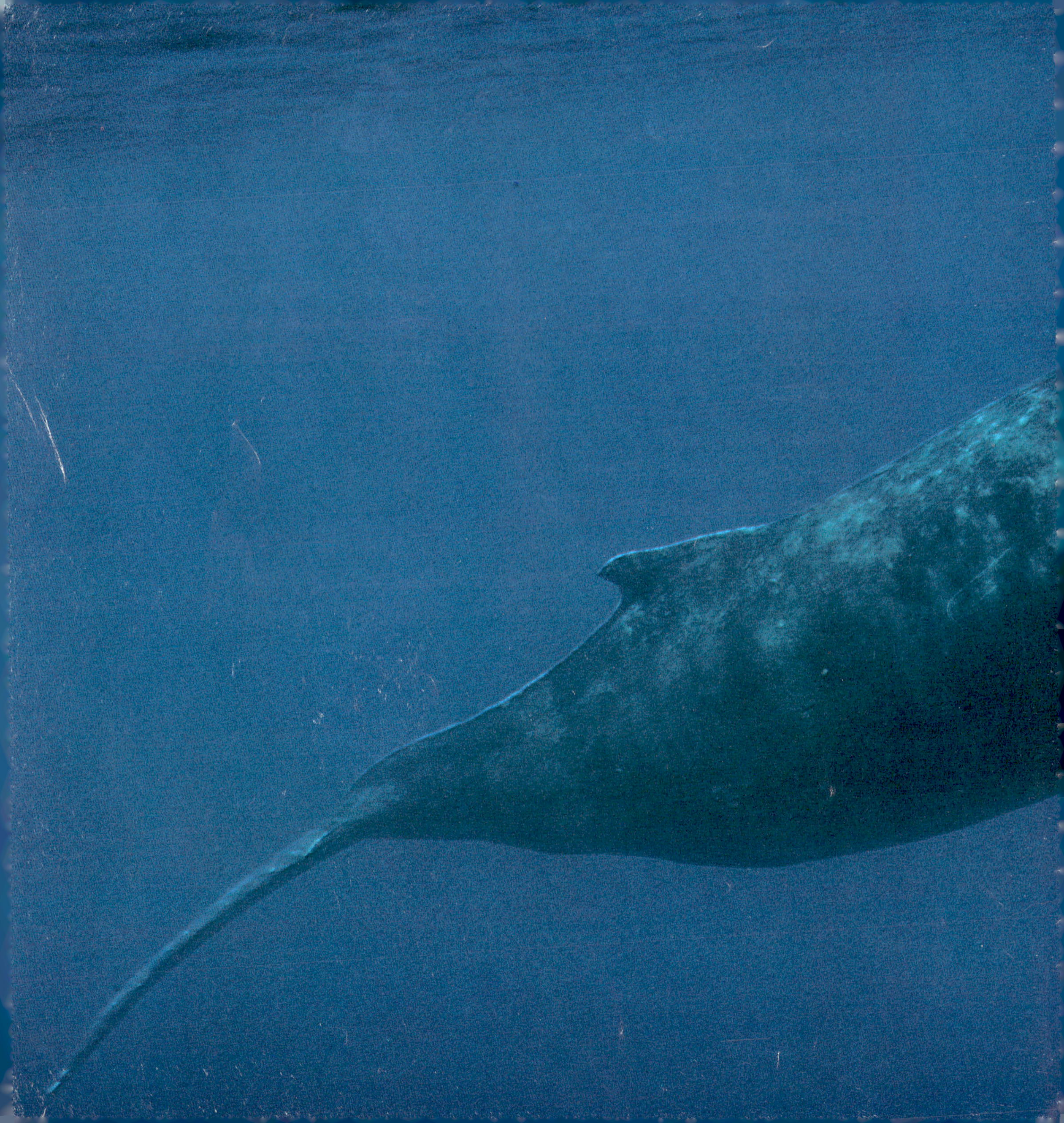

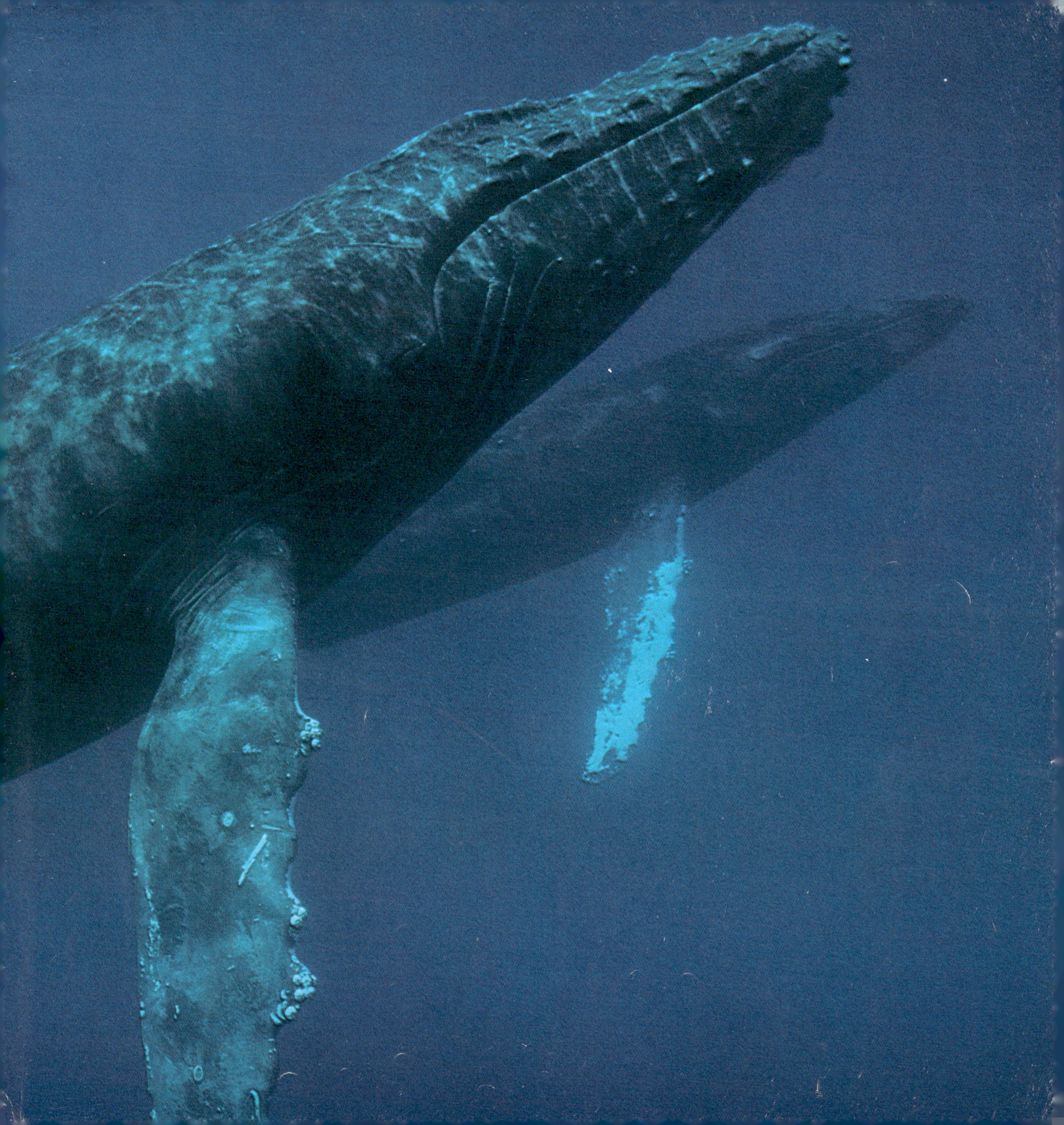

Humpback Whale:
Maximum length - 50 feet
Weight - 45 tons (90,000 lbs.)

Characteristics: The humpback whale gets its name from a humped roll of fat on its back. The humpback whale has many *barnacles* and *crustaceans* on its body. It has large flippers, 12-13 feet long, used for navigation. The humpback whale is dark in color with white patches on its underside. It is found in all oceans.

Gray Whale:

Maximum length - 60 feet
Weight - 40 tons (80,000 lbs.)

Characteristics: The gray whale has a low ridge on its back in place of a fin. It is dark gray or black with many white spots and barnacles on its head. The gray whale is found in the north Pacific region.

Right Whale:

Maximum length - 60 feet
Weight - 50 tons (100,000 lbs.)

Characteristics: The right whale has a "horny" bonnet on its snout and a very large head. It has short, broad flippers. The right whale is black. It may be found in all oceans.

Bowhead Whale:

Maximum length - 55 feet
Weight - 45 tons (90,000 lbs.)

Characteristics: The bowhead whale looks very much like a right whale but it does not have a bonnet on its snout. The bowhead whale is black and is found in the Arctic.

GLOSSARY

The words below also appear in the text in *italicized* type. The page number on which each word first appears is listed after each definition.

Adapt: To adjust or conform to a new way of living (page 29).

Artiodactyls: A group of hoofed land mammals (for example, antelope, caribou, pigs, or moose) with an even number of functioning toes (page 30).

Barnacles: Various small crustacean marine animals that form a hard shell and cling to submerged surfaces (page 44).

Blubber: A whale's fat (page 14).

Condense: (for water vapor) to become liquid (page 23).

Crustaceans: Aquatic animals that have no bones or skeleton, but a shell and two pairs of antennae (page 44).

Estuary: A bay or river mouth where salt water from the ocean meets fresh water (page 27).

Extinction: The condition that occurs when all members of a species no longer exist (page 27).

Flippers: The "arms" of a whale, used for turning (page 11).

Fluke: The tail of a whale, used for swimming (page 17).

Mammals: Animals that have spinal cords and that nurse their young with milk (page 5).

Mesonychids: The earliest group of mammals (page 27).

Origins: The beginning point at which something exists (page 27).

Plankton: Very tiny organisms that drift on the surface of the ocean (page 40).

Suffocate: To die from lack of air (page 21).

ADULT-CHILD INTERACTION QUESTIONS

These are questions you may ask young readers to get them to think about whales as viable occupants of a niche in the food chain. Encourage them to explain their feelings about whales and to ask their own questions. Clarify any misunderstandings they may have about the predator-prey relationship as it relates to whales, and explain the need to have both predators and prey in the world. In this way, you can help foster future generations of environmentally aware and appreciative adults. More information about whales is available in the Gareth Stevens title The Story of Three Whales, *a factual account of three whales trapped in icy Alaskan waters.*

1. The whale is the largest animal that has ever lived. Does this mean that it is safe from any kind of natural enemies?

2. You know that whales are mammals. Name some characteristics of mammals.

3. Whales live in family groups. Why do you think this is good for the whales?

4. We know that mother whales, like human mothers, hug their babies. What other things do you think whales do that humans do?

5. Do you think it would be fun to be a whale? Why?